THE
CAGEBIRDS

A Play

DAVID CAMPTON

SAMUEL  FRENCH

LONDON
NEW YORK TORONTO SYDNEY HOLLYWOOD

ISBN 0 573 03366 8

CAST

The Long-Tongued Gossip

The Mirror-Eyed Gazer

The Medicated Gloom

The Regular Thump

The Constant Twitting

The Great Guzzler

The Wild One

The Mistress

The action takes place in a room with a single large door

NOTE

Although no character is based on a specific bird, they could have bird-like characteristics, particularly in movement. Bird-like appendages could be translated into human terms: there need be no beaks or plumage, but a long beak, for instance, could be indicated by a walking-stick, or extravagant plumage by a fan.

Although each bird seems to have its own particular song, the intent behind the words should be made plain. It is possible to say "pass the salt" aggressively, longingly, with passion or fear: so with these speeches, even though the meaning of the scene cuts across the words.

THE CAGEBIRDS

A room with a large, locked door

Several Ladies sit or stand around the room. This could almost be a committee meeting, except for the fact that each lady is totally absorbed in her own thoughts

There is a long, long, pause.

Suddenly The Thump, in response to some brooded-upon indignity, says "Huh!" very loudly. Then she is lost in her thoughts again

Pause

The Gazer gets out a compact mirror, and looks at herself in it—almost as though she needed urgent reassurance that her face was still there. She touches a curl or smooths an eyebrow, then puts the mirror away again

Pause

The Twitting clears her throat as though about to say something, then changes her mind

The Gloom puts a hand to her forehead, and sighs

The Gossip has a sudden intake of breath as of someone receiving dire and important news

The Guzzle burps

Then there is a pause again

All of which, in entirely human terms, should try to suggest the occasional tweets and shuffles of birds roosting

Gossip So she said to me . . .

Slight pause

Gloom Camphorated oil.

Slight pause

Gazer Rinse and set.
Guzzle With double cream.
Thump Disgusting.
Twitting I don't know, I'm sure.
Thump ⎱ Ugh! ⎰ (*Speaking together*)
Gazer ⎰ Ah! ⎱
Guzzle ⎱ Not forgetting the cherry on top.
Gossip ⎰ All of which is a matter of opinion. ⎱ (*Speaking
Gloom ⎰ What else can I expect at my age? ⎰ *together*)
Twitting I don't know. I really don't know.

*Pause. The Thump gets up; strides to the other side of the room;
looks around with mingled suspicion and aggression; then strides
back and assumes her original position as though nothing had
happened*

Gloom (*suddenly, to no-one in particular*) It's the knee, you know.
It locks. Rigid. (*She sticks her leg out in front of her to demon-
strate*) In the most awkward places—where one hesitates to
call a boy scout for assistance. Even supposing a boy scout
happened to be handy. And the chances of one having a
first-aid badge are astronomically against. What use is wood-
craft when dealing with a locked knee-cap? It's the cap that's
responsible, of course. The cap. This. The lining wears.
Lubrication helps from time to time. Embrocation. Rubbed
in with vigour. But can one ask a boy scout to embrocate
with vigour? After the home help refused. "Table legs, yes"
was the reply. "Other legs, no." She advised an elastic bandage.
"Only the angels know what a comfort my elastic bandage
has been," she told me. But when a knee-cap locks, it locks.
There's no permanent relief short of amputation. One hesitates
to have one's knees removed. There's nothing for the rest of
the leg to hang on to without the knee. Who'd sacrifice half
a leg to a locked knee-cap? Not that there's much to lose—
corns, bunions, ingrowing toe-nails, fallen arches, athlete's
foot. Legs are a trouble from one end to the other. Yet one
hangs on to them. For sentimental reasons, I suppose. They
have supported one. Except when the knee locked. (*She sub-
sides, thinking about knee-caps*)
Twitting You'll have to put me down among the "don't knows".
Thump Organization. That's what's lacking. I'll organize 'em,

The Guzzle and The Gazer appear to converse with each other. In ping-pong dialogue one makes a statement and the other seems to respond to it. It just happens that they are talking about different subjects

Guzzle Gravy is most important.

Gazer Oh, indeed. Never back-brush too hard.

Guzzle Dark brown and smooth it should be.

Gazer That's what I tell them. There's no point in spending a small fortune on a permanent if you brush it all out again.

Guzzle Exactly. How can bumps get into the gravy? Criminal carelessness.

Gazer Not that I expect a permanent to be too permanent.

Guzzle No, indeed. There's no excuse for lumps.

Gazer This year's fashion is next year's old hat. But I have such fine hair.

Guzzle Even in times of economic stress my gravy was exemplary.

Gazer Mine is like spun gossamer.

Guzzle Speaking as a consumer.

Gazer Bobby pins tomorrow.

Guzzle A gravy user.

Gazer With gossamer.

Guzzle Gravy.

Gazer What there is of it.

Twitting I was never given to opinions.

The Thump rises and strikes an attitude as though about to deliver an important announcement, then changes her mind, and sinks down again. The Gossip stands

Gossip No use coming to me with your tales, I told her. I'm not one of your lines of communication. I really don't know where she gets it all. Though I've seen her myself with an ear to the bedroom wall. Don't ask me how, because I've never been one to divulge a source of information. A secret with me is as safe as the graveyard. Not like some people we know. We've seen their telescopes, haven't we? And their periscopes. To say nothing of gyroscopes, microscopes, and thermometers. We know who conveys those tasty titbits from keyhole to keyhole. Don't look at me. I'm not one of your talkers. You won't catch me hanging round the cooked-meat counter. I keep myself to myself—which is the safest place when all's said and done. *Honi soit qui mal y pense.* You've heard that one, haven't you? Of course you have. I'm always coming out with it. It's from the French. Not that I'm given to the French. Not like someone we all know. It's in *her* blood. You don't have to take my word for it; you can see by the way she carries on. Oh, I could tell you a tale or two. I know. (*She returns to her place*)

Twitting Don't ask me. Please.

The Mistress's voice is heard off. Ideally this would be an amplified whisper

Mistress (*off*) Sweeties. Sweeties, sweeties, sweeties.

The Ladies look at each other, then immediately try to appear as though they had not

(*Off*) Where are my sweeties?

The Ladies get up and move about rapidly, but aimlessly—talking, but never listening

Guzzle Surely it must be tea-time. Where are the muffins and crumpets? Where are the toasted tea-cakes? Where is the thin-cut bread and butter? Where is the tea?

Gloom Warm wrapping. That's the only answer. Lagging, if you look at it from the plumber's point of view. Why should we cosset our pipes, but neglect our torsos? Medicated wool is the answer. Yards of it.

Gazer I've been experimenting with underwater shades—pearl, coral, and anemone. Youthful tints. Far too youthful to be left to mere youth. Pearl, and coral, and sea something. Has anyone noticed?

Gossip Only one leg. That's a fact. I heard it myself. That makes you think, doesn't it? Someone has some explaining to do if you ask me. All those years and only one leg.

Thump The rot must be stopped. That's what a dentist does with a decaying tooth. He stops it. This is a decaying society. It must be stopped before the rot spreads.

Twitting This is all so unsettling. Nothing stays the same for more than two seconds running. Even the barometer goes up and down like clockwork. How can one trust in anything when everything is always changing?

Pause. There is the amplified sound of a key being turned in a lock
The Ladies move about and talk even faster

Guzzle Tea-cakes. Tea-cakes. Tea-cakes. Cream buns and puff-
paste. Tea. Tea. Tea.

Gloom Warm. Warmer. Warmest. Wrap up. Avoid draughts.
Keep warm. Warmer. Warmest.

Gazer Beautiful for ever. Health and beauty. Home and beauty.
Sleep. Beauty. Sleep.

Gossip No. No. Not a word. Listen to this. Did you ever? No,
no.

Thump Stop. Stop. Stop. Down with it. Out with it. Away with
it. Stop. Stop. Stop.

Twitting Not again. Oh, not again. This is too much. Much too
much. Not again.

The door is opened. Everyone stands very still, very quiet

> *The Mistress stands in the doorway. She is a smiling and benign,*
> *but authoritative person, older than the Ladies, and, if possible,*
> *taller than any of them*

Mistress Here are my sweeties. (*She shuts the door behind her and*
advances into the room) How are my sweeties?

The Ladies move about again, but in turn come up to the Mistress

Twittering It's the uncertainty that bothers me. If only I could
be sure about anything. But I'm not. One day I think one way,
and the next day I think the opposite.

Mistress That's because you're a permanently floating voter.

Twitting Am I? Am I really? Oh, thank you so much.

Thump Sex and violence. You've seen it, haven't you? Even in
comics. I've made a study of comics. Lurid with lust and bad
jokes. It's a problem.

Mistress But in such safe hands.

Thump The censor. That's what we need. Bring back the censor.

Gloom Have you been innoculated against rabies?

Mistress Against everything.

Gloom How wise.

Gossip Have you heard?

Mistress Whisper.

The Gossip does so

Mistress Incredible.

Gossip Nothing but the truth.

Gazer Have you noticed?

Mistress Beautiful.

Gazer I think so, too.

Mistress And I have something for my pet Guzzle. (*She hands Guzzle a macaroon*)

Guzzle A macaroon? I was just thinking about a macaroon. I shall keep it always to remind me of you. (*She eats it*)

The Mistress claps her hands. The Ladies react with gasps, squeaks, and snorts according to their nature

Mistress Listen.

The Ladies listen

You have a new playmate. You will be kind to her, won't you?

Gazer It's this light. Not the kindest to my complexion.

Mistress I know you will. You'll have to be specially understanding because she is a Wild One. Her little ways may not be your little ways. But I know you'll be understanding.

Gloom I wonder if it isn't all in the mind.

Mistress Remember when I first introduced our little Twitting.

Twitting I would if I could, but . . .

Mistress You made her at home almost at once.

Guzzle Why is it impossible to get old-fashioned tripe and onions?

Mistress So I know you'll all do your best for our Wild One.

Gossip I've heard. I'm passing nothing on, you understand. But I've heard.

Mistress I know, my sweeties. Just a minute while I fetch your new companion. Isn't this exciting?

The Mistress goes out, shutting the door after her

Thump Wild? Wild? The magistrates aren't severe enough. Let off with a caution instead of the cat.

Guzzle Wild things are oppressively expensive. Rice. Strawberries. Because they are luxuries. Are they luxuries because they're expensive, or are they expensive because they're luxuries?

Mistress (*off*) This way, my sweet.
Thump Wild.
Guzzle Rice.
Gossip Paper.
Gazer Hat.
Gloom Stand.
Twitting Aside.

The door opens and The Mistress ushers in The Wild One. The Wild One is possibly a little younger than the others. What really distinguishes her from them, though, is her attitude. She is receptive to what is going on around her

Wild One So this is my prison.
Mistress Your home.
Wild One My cage.
Mistress We don't use that word. Look, everyone. Here is your new friend.

The Ladies want to turn and look at the newcomer, but this is not done. They steal little sidelong glances, and then pretend that they have not. They continue to suffer from curiosity, and to fall for temptation

You'll be happy here.
Wild One Is that an order?
Mistress I know you'll be happy here.
Wild One I was happy there.
Mistress You would have died. You have enemies out there— predators whose first impulse is to tear you to pieces.
Wild One And what happens to me here?
Mistress You'll be looked after. Protected. I'm your friend.
Wild One First rule for any prisoner: make sure the gaoler is a friend.
Mistress Please don't be unhappy.
Wild One Are these happy?
Mistress They are contented.
Wild One A different word. For locks read apathy, for bolts resignation; and the bars are called contentment. I warned you —I shall escape.
Mistress And I warned you. Your choice is life or death. Do be

a sensible creature. You'll soon settle down. Won't she, my sweeties? All so cosy.

Wild One I won't call you mistress.

Mistress It isn't compulsory.

Wild One I won't perform for you.

Mistress You amuse me just as you are.

Wild One I don't sing or dance or make jokes. I'm not pretty and I'm not loving. Why have you brought me here?

Mistress Perhaps I feel sorry for you.

Wild One Charity! That's a great luxury. I hate you for it.

Mistress That's up to you, my pet. Your frost can never kill my satisfaction.

Wild One Leave me, then. If you won't release me, leave me.

Mistress I always try to do what is best for my sweeties. (*She goes to the door*) I'm sorry I have to lock the door. It's for the best. For all of you.

The Mistress goes out. There is the amplified sound of the key turning in the lock

The Wild One suddenly turns, runs up to the door, and tries to open it. It is securely locked. The Wild One beats at it with her fists. The Ladies stare ahead, a little distressed by this display of emotion, but determined to show nothing themselves. The Wild One stops beating the door. Slowly she turns and looks at the Ladies. Silence, which goes on until The Wild One has to break it

Wild One I'm sorry. I—hope I—didn't upset you. (*Pause*) These performances must be disturbing. I'm in full control of myself now. (*Pause*) I'm sorry if I behaved stupidly. (*With voice rising*) But I am not used to walls, and ceilings, and doors with locks. (*She checks herself*) Sorry.

Silence. The Wild One ventures a little farther into the room

(*With a slight, rueful smile*) I have to make myself at home. Command from on high . . . I'm your new cage companion. (*Pause*) Shall we get acquainted? I may not be here for long. (*Pause*) I shouldn't be here at all, but I was given no choice. There has been a miscarriage of justice. (*She checks herself*)

Silence

But you probably know about that. After all, you're here yourselves.

Silence. The Wild One walks about the room, looking at The Ladies, who pretend they are not being looked at

(*Becoming irritated*) What happened when you were first put here? Did you go into a cataleptic trance? Did you go off your pet food? Did you squeal with your heels in the air? Or did you sing sweetly from the minute the door slammed? (*She realizes that she is shouting*) I'm sorry.

Silence. The Wild One returns to the centre of the room

I'm sorry. I shouldn't be here. I know I shouldn't be here. But what can I do? I'm sorry.

Silence

Up the Revolution! Votes for Women! Take me to your Leader!

Silence

I'm sorry. You were here first. You call the tune. You chose your own time. I don't understand your rules. I don't know any rules. Check. I know one. There should be no cages. But here we are in a cage. What good is the rest of the rule-book when the first rule is broken? (*She checks herself*) I'm sorry. (*Pause*) I expect you'll be hearing that a lot. As long as I'm here. As long as . . .

Silence. The Wild One waits. She notices The Twitting's head turn ever so slightly as she steals a peep. The Wild One strides over to the Twitting

(*Aggressively*) So you're contented, are you?
Twitting I—er—I—don't—er—know.
Wild One That's better. At least one of you knows I'm here.
Twitting I shouldn't be asked. I'm not ready to give an opinion
Wild One What about the rest?

Pause

I'm trying to understand you. (*She turns to The Guzzle*) You
Guzzle Why are sucking-pigs suddenly out of fashion?
Wild One Why are what—what?

Guzzle There's no delicacy quite like a roast sucking-pig. Some people object and say that it looks like a baby in the dish, but I've never seen a roast baby, so I wouldn't know. I've seen a roast sucking-pig. Ah! Love at first sight.

Wild One You did say . . .

Guzzle I hope no-one roasts babies.

Wild One But . . . (*She backs away from The Guzzle, and bumps into The Thump*)

Thump Too many long-haired louts about.

Wild One Do you think . . . ?

Thump And short-haired sex fiends. Stiff prison sentences—they're the only answer.

Wild One You can't mean that.

Thump And hanging, of course.

The Wild One turns away from her

They should never have done away with the gibbet.

Gloom It all began with an ache in the little finger. But it was neglected. An ache in the little finger should never be neglected. It spread. At last she fell down the steps at St Paul's, and died on the spot. Broken neck.

Wild One You're not talking to me, are you?

Gloom Never neglect a little finger.

Wild One Not one of you is talking to me

Gazer Personally I think there is a lot to be said for cerulean blue over the eyelids.

Wild One Not one.

Gossip You won't let it go any further? After all, a confidence is a confidence.

Wild One Not one. (*She puts her hands to her head, and shuts her eyes tightly*)

Pause. The Thump glances at The Wild One, then takes a tentative step towards her

The Thump rapidly turns away

Just. . . . Don't. . . . Understand. (*She looks about her again*) I mean—you're not just mechanical things that operate when the penny drops.

Guzzle I have a cookery book by my bedside. Then I'm sure to dream of food. Not the same cookery book every night, of course—even a dream banquet grows tedious without variety. Smoked salmon repeated often enough would become a bore. Imagine smoked salmon becoming a nightmare. That's a nightmare.

Wild One What does that mean? You're using words, but I don't understand.

Gloom It's the stomach—for want of a better word. Upheavals even after bismuth. Bile coming up again and again. Only a sufferer knows what I suffer.

Wild One I don't understand you. I try, but . . .

Gossip I was nowhere near at the time of the accident. But I can put two and two together. If the cap fits . . .

Gazer Never laugh, and never frown. That's the way to avoid wrinkles.

Wild One Please. I'm trying to evaluate the situation.

Thump A petition. That's the only answer. Come to me if you need signatures.

Wild One All right. Let me try to put myself in your place. How long have you been here? Days? Weeks? Months? Years? Have you always been here? Are you content to sit as time slips by—all the days, weeks, months, years to come? She said you're content. Perhaps you are. But if you are it's because you never . . . Doesn't anything matter to you beyond aches and food, scandal and the reflection in your mirror? Isn't there room for anything in your mind but prejudice and fear? You're oppressed and you don't even notice the fact. You are denied your basic human rights, and you don't even care. You are prisoners. Are you content with that? I'm just trying to understand you, that's all. Just trying. Did you ever behave like me? Did you ever beat at the door, shout protest slogans? Complain about the injustice of it all? Or shall I, given time, become like you—secure in my own little space, perhaps working out endless, beautiful, complicated, useless plans for escape? Never! Listen to me. You are going to listen to me. (*She goes up to The Gossip and holds her arm*) Listen. The world stretches farther than the few inches between your ears.

Gossip Nobody ever accused me of spreading slander. I always check my facts.

Wild One There is another world outside.

Gossip Tell the truth and shame the devil. So I was taught.

(*She breaks away from The Wild One*)

The Wild One goes to The Gloom, and holds her arm

Wild One Listen. We are going to escape. You, me, and all the others.

Gloom If you've never suffered from sinus, there's no point in trying to explain.

Wild One A door is only a door. Enough hands can break it down.

Gloom The tubes! (*She breaks away from The Wild One*)

The Wild One goes to The Gazer

Wild One Listen. We are a majority.

Gazer Deep cleansing is the answer. Free the pores. Let the skin breathe.

Wild One It's not even a question of democracy: it's a matter of numbers. There are seven of us to one of her. She is not only outvoted, she is outnumbered.

Gazer Witchhazel. (*She removes The Wild One's hand from her arm, and walks away*)

Wild One (*shouting*) Listen to me! All of you! You could be free. All of you! Must I be caged because you lack willpower? (*She pauses, and looks around her. She gives a rueful little laugh*) I have no right, have I? No right to commit such an outrage.

She goes up to one of the Ladies who, at the last minute, moves away—not obviously or insultingly, but as though she had just remembered that she ought to be somewhere else. Through the following speech this pattern is repeated, so the room is full of Ladies weaving about, without The Wild One getting too close to any of them

I come bursting in—actually I was tossed in, but let that pass. I come hurtling in, and within minutes turn your comfortable, satisfied, non-communicating, slave society upside down. I tear down the paper screens you built so carefully. I blow great gusts through the hot-house air. I shatter your fragile Sunday quiet, No, I didn't I only tried. I didn't succeed. I couldn't succeed, because you're not alive. You can't be alive, because if you were, you'd be charging at that door with me. This very minute. All shoulders together. Boom! Thud! Pow! Crash! But there you sit. I haven't the right to stir the dust. I'm the Wild One who doesn't belong. Ignore her. You have to ignore her, because if you didn't you'd either have to break out or break down. I'm sorry. No, I'm not, but it's an accepted figure of speech. I'm sorry, but if you don't like me, you'll have to do the other thing. I'm sorry, but I'm the Wild One, and the cage hasn't been built that can hold me. (*She takes a long run at the door, and hurls herself at it with such force that she bounces off. The impact whirls her round until she collapses in a heap*)

Pause. The Guzzle looks at her, then quickly looks away again. The Gazer looks at her, and shrugs her shoulders. The Gossip looks at her, takes a step towards her, then thinks better of it. The Gloom goes up to her, shrugs her shoulders, and returns. The Thump goes up to her, shakes her head, and returns. The Twitting goes up to her, wrings her hands, and looks around helplessly. The Wild One looks up. The Twitting squeals and freezes, slightly behind The Wild One, and, she hopes, out of sight

That wasn't the way. (*She gets up and finds herself face to face with The Twitting*)

Hullo.

Twitting I'd rather not say.

The Twitting tries to tiptoe away from The Wild One, but The Wild One follows. Whatever twists and turns The Twitting takes The Wild One is always there. As the other Ladies see what is happening they become disturbed. They actually look at each other. They move towards each other. They bunch together

Wild One I said "hullo".

Twitting I never give an opinion.

Wild One That's trying to be friendly.

Twitting I don't even vote.

Wild One I wouldn't make you do anything you didn't want to do. Not even say "hullo".

Twitting I'm not responsible.

Wild One I might try to persuade you, but that's different. Anyone is open to persuasion. Anyone who listens.

Twitting I haven't made up my mind.

Wild One And you're listening.

Twitting I am not listening.

Wild One Hurrah! Someone is listening.

Twitting You must ask someone else.

Wild One You may pretend, but you can't help yourself.

Twitting Questions confuse me.

Wild One I'm sorry to pick on you, because you're so easily frightened, but a beginning has to be made somewhere.

Twitting There are so many answers to the simplest question.

Wild One I'm sorry to pick on you, because it makes me feel such a bully.

Twitting No answer.

Wild One But listen.

Twitting Gone away.

Wild One I just want to tell you about out there.

Twitting Address unknown.

Wild One Do you remember out there?

Twitting Return to sender.

Wild One Were you ever out there?

Twitting I can't.

Wild One Out there where the wind blows and the sun shines. Where heat and light and air have nothing to do with central heating or electric lamps or air conditioning. Do you remember the wind? It tickles and it buffets; it sighs and it roars; it swoops suddenly from the north tearing trees in its path; then, just as suddenly, it changes into a whisper from the south, rustling in the grass. That's the wind. Can you live without it? Of course you can—as long as you can forget about it.

Twitting I won't.

Wild One I'm reminding you again. I don't want to hurt you. But does it hurt so much to remember? Do you remember the clouds? Little white puffs against a wash of blue; great, grey mountains piling up until they crash in thunder; fiery streamers of flame and gold blazing across the sky in the hallelujah of a sunset. The clouds. Remember them? Those high-borne miracles. Remember?

Twitting I daren't.

Wild One You must remember. Remember the winter. Yes, even the frost. When every pool became a mirror and every spray a crystal cluster. When the earth set rock hard, and each day was a test with bare life the prize at the end. When owls hooted at the frozen moon, and hawks plummeted down the thin air. Yes, remember even hunger and death. But can you remember that and be content with this?

The Twitting has now backed into a corner from which there is no escape

Twitting No!
Wild One Remember!
Twitting No! No!! No!!! (*She sinks to the ground and curls up with her hands over her ears*)
Wild One Don't you want to escape—even into memories? Please. Unwind. I'm trying to help. I want to set you free. (*Pause*) That wasn't the way either. (*She kneels beside The Twitting*) Where did I fail? Am I too articulate? Should I have limited my words, scaled down my imagination to your mind. I can't. I would if I could because I want to reach you. But I can't. You're all out of reach. (*She stands up, turns away from The Twitting, and sees The Ladies*)

They are all together in a tight semi-circle on the opposite side of the room, staring at The Wild One

What's this? A delegation? An investigation? A confrontation?

The Ladies glance uneasily at each other

But you're all together. Shoulder to shoulder. What wrought this miracle?

Pause

Could it have been me? You're looking at me. You can see me. I exist. I cause a reaction, therefore I exist. Is this a breakthrough? Glory be! It's a breakthrough. We're communicating.

Pause

And the next move?

Pause

Come on now. Make the most of our new-found togetherness.
Who's for tennis?

Pause

Will you all join me? A crusade, anyone? Shall we form up
behind the banner, singing out the battle-cry of freedom?
Shall we shout down the walls of Jericho?

Pause

I'm jumping the gun, aren't I? I'm pushing my luck. I'm running before I can walk. Am I going too far? Yes, I am. And
I'm going farther. I'll lead you all into the Promised Land.

*The Twitting has slowly raised her head to see what is going on.
As The Wild One turns, The Twitting ducks down again with a
squeak*

Yes, even you. You're coming with me. We'll smell the wild
thyme together. See that door? We're going through it. (*She
goes up to the door. She feels over its surface*) It's only a door—
an artifact of wood and metal. A dead thing. I'm alive. I
can think. A door can't think. So all the advantages are on
my side. There's a way through. There's always a way through.
Through or under or round. Where there's a door, there's a
way out. (*She peers through the keyhole*)

*The Ladies do not know what is going to happen next, and ner-
vously talk among themselves*

Guzzle (*after nervously clearing her throat*) I always said that
apple pie should be served with cinnamon.
Gloom Cinnamon is good for colds and other infections. Ask
any doctor.
Gossip The doctor could tell you. My word, yes. He knows how
many they sleep to a bed.
Gazer A bed-time face-pack. I swear by it.
Thump Such profanity should be stopped. Who knows where it
may end? It should be stopped.

The Wild One turns round

Wild One What should be stopped?
Thump I know what I know. (*She turns away*)

Wild One I know this lock. It can be opened. I need a hairpin. Who has a hairpin?

The Ladies turn away. The Wild One goes to The Gazer

Hairpin?

Gazer I have a mirror. And a powder puff. (*She scurries away from The Wild One*)

Wild One You.

Gossip Don't say I told you. (*She slips away and joins The Gazer*)

Wild One You, then.

Gloom They're no good for pains in the chest. (*She hurries to The Gazer and The Gossip*)

Wild One You, or you.

Guzzle Cheese-cake. It's such a long time since I tasted real cheese-cake. (*Rapt with her vision of food she drifts over to the others*)

Thump Huh! (*She stumps behind The Guzzle*)

Wild One All I need is a hairpin. A piece of bent wire. A hairpin.

The Twitting stares at her. The Wild One stares at The Twitting. The Twitting pulls something from her hair and holds it out at arm's length. Slowly The Wild One goes over to her and takes it

Thank you.

Twitting I don't know. I—really . . . (*She turns away and covers her face with her hands*)

The Wild One goes up to the door. While The Wild One kneels in front of the door, working on the lock, the Ladies are all aflutter. They make little nervous movements, sometimes sneaking up behind The Wild One and peeping over her shoulder, sometimes taking a completely aimless turn around the room. At one point The Thump comes down to The Twitter and pulls her into the group. All the time they chatter, chatter, chatter. Sometimes they address each other. Sometimes they talk at the same time. Sometimes they start to address one person and end by talking to another. Sometimes they talk to themselves. For the sake of convenience, all this is written down as one speech per person

Guzzle I can remember my schoolday meals. Cooking has declined since then. Boiled suet puddings oozing with jam and

thick, yellow custard over everything. I could eat three help-
ings of suet puddings in those days: now I can hardly manage
one. Does nobody know how to cook a suet pudding? I remember toffee apples and aniseed balls and sherbert dabs. Satin
cushions that exploded into fizz, and yards of coiled liquorice.
Of course sweets were strictly for between meals, along with
green gooseberries, hard sour apples, and sticks of rhubarb.
At mealtimes there were snowy mounds of potato, golden
crusts yielding a gush of steak and kidney. And the joy of
scraping a dish or picking at a marrow bone . . . Why does
nothing taste so good any more? Whence has the freshness and
delicacy gone? Is it the frozen foods? Is it adulterated ferti-
lizers? Is it chemical additives to the feeding-stuffs? Or has
the art of cooking been forgotten? I can remember making
toffee over my grandmother's stove. Half the mixture was lost
on the cooker, and a quarter in my hair. But I have never
tasted toffee like it since. Nor sage and onion stuffing for that
matter. My grandmother made glorious sage and onion
stuffing. It repeated and repeated and repeated. I can taste it
now. Or wish I could. You could keep all your oysters and
turtle soup for . . . Turtle soup! Ah!

Gazer I believe that if a woman has assets, it is worth her while
to make the most of them. And if her assets should happen
to be sub-standard—well, it is up to her to build them up.
I can say that there have never been any complaints about
my assets. But I have always been aware of them, and dis-
played them in the best light. It is nonsense to say that one's
assets decline as the years roll by. One's assets are as good as
the care one takes of them. After all, we all know what tremen-
dous work goes on back-stage, but we forget it from the moment
the curtain goes up. My assets and I are old friends. And so
they should be, considering what has been lavished upon them.
I have never believed in hidden assets. Hinted at—yes, if the
performance is likely to fall short of the promise: but never
completely concealed.

Gloom It all starts with a tightness in the chest. A tightness in
the chest can develop into anything. Let it rise to the head, and
you have a head-ache. Let it sink to the stomach, and you
have the stomach-ache. Let it fly to the heart, and you have
the heart-ache. Let it penetrate to the back, and you've got

back-ache, which farther down turns into piles. Don't let them tell you that piles are started by sitting on hot radiators or cold stones. I have never sat on a hot radiator or cold stone in my life, but what I've suffered from piles is a secret between myself, and . . . Piles begin through neglecting a pain in the chest. I know, because I've had it. Only those who've had it know what it is. I've sat there in the middle of the night, afraid to breathe for the tightness in my chest. Tightness in the chest has brought me close to suffocation. Nothing brings permanent relief. I've tried menthol. I've tried chlorodyne. I've tried vinegar rags, hot fomentations, and kaolin poultices. They work for a while, and then . . . Tightness in the chest has more deaths to its credit than any other disease. Yet the doctors refuse to believe in it. Because it doesn't have a Latin name, they refuse to give it credence. Thrombosis, they put on the certificate. Compound fractures, they say. Nicotine poisoning. What do they know? They've never had it. A Middle-Eastern friend of mine recommended camel-dung. But where is one to find a camel in this country? I was laughed at when I took a bucket and spade to Whipsnade.

Thump I've never called a spade anything but a spade. But the place for a spade is the tool-shed, and not the middle of the drawing-room carpet. We're all human beings; we know how human beings behave; and we know that, for half the time, that behaviour is pretty disgusting—eating, drinking, sleeping, and so on. But there is no need to have such so-on thrust at us in the name of permissive entertainment. Last night, barely had the set warmed up, than we were regaled with the exhibition of a person peeling a banana. No need to mention the network. We all know. That network is manned exclusively by Catholics, Communists, Jews, Freemasons, Freethinkers, libertines, homosexuals, warmongers, and pacifists. We also know—and this is a fact—that the switchboard of that network was jammed with protesting calls for several hours after the peeling of that offending fruit. We have our network, too. And it is showing results. Within our lifetime we can look forward to entertainment devoid of any content whatsoever. But the cause needs effort. Petitions and protests. Write to your M.P. Write to your local council. Write to your newspaper, your banker, your solicitor. Write again and again.

Provoke the opposition into hitting back. Remember—a suc-
cessful libel action is worth a dozen collecting boxes.

Gossip You don't have to believe me. It's happened before, and
it'll happen again. They can't keep a thing like that to themselves. Well, could you? It stands to reason. It's crying out.
Not that I ever interfered. If that's the way they want to carry
on, then let them. But don't let them come to me when it's all
over. Oh, my goodness, the things I'll say if they do . . .
"You wouldn't listen to me," I'll tell them. "Experience tells,"
I'll throw at them. I've never been one to . . . And you know
it. Let them spread all the tales they like. You may very well
ask. There's no answer without a question. No smoke without
fire. And they'll realize it before they're much older. I mean—
there's a limit, isn't there? You can see it, can't you? A limit.
Plain enough without anybody having to point it out. Not that
I ever interfered. I'm not the interfering sort. "Get on with it,"
I'll say. "Get on with it. And may Heaven forgive you."

Twitting Perhaps I shouldn't have. I never did before. Perhaps
I never shall again. It was an impulse. Never give way to
impulses. That's a rule. I never have rules. I don't know what
came over me. I really don't know. Should I have done that?
Was it right or wrong? Never do anything that you have to
ask yourself. Right or wrong? What is right? What is wrong?
Right yesterday is wrong today. And vice versa. Never make
decisions. I made a decision. Oh, Lord, forgive us our decisions.
Don't let it count against me. I'll rub it out. Cancel it. Reverse
it. But that means another decision, and I never make decisions. I leave decisions to other people. Let them fill up their
questionnaires. Let them make their crosses and drip them into
the ballot box. Whatever happens is no concern of mine. I
have no effect on the course of events. I was not responsible.
I disdain all responsibility. For what may happen hereafter.
Just leave me alone, everyone. Alone. I never listen to mani-
festos because they confuse me. I am the permanently floating
voter. The permanent floater.

Wild One Ah!

*The chatter stops instantly as though cut with a knife. The door
swings open. The Wild One stands up. For a few seconds she stares
out into the open space. Then she turns to the others*

(*Ecstatically*) Lettest. In peace. Now. Depart.

The Ladies silently move together and form a compact group

I promised it could be done. Any door can be opened. Any prison can be broken. We can go now. Follow me.

The Wild One turns and hurries through the door

The Ladies move as far as possible from the door, then stand still. Pause

The Wild One returns

Come on. There's no time to waste. She'll soon be back to her sweeties. The cage must be empty by then. Hurry! (*She turns to go but realizes that the Ladies are static*) Don't you understand? You're free. Once through that door there's nothing between you and the stars. Why are you holding back? Look. No door. I'm giving you your freedom. Why aren't you taking it? Are you waiting for an official proclamation? Can't you realize? Here's the gateway to the universe. Waiting for the idea to sink in? Waiting's a luxury we can't afford. Soon the damage is going to be discovered. Good-bye to simple locks after that. Tomorrow there'll be bolts and bars, balls and chains, portcullis and drawbridge. It's now or never. We must move. Move! Move! Why won't you move? Is the prospect of liberty too much for you? Or are you just—afraid? You are. You are. I'm offering the world, and you're afraid to take it.

Pause

I see. Then I'll go without you. You don't deserve a second thought.

The Wild One goes out

The Ladies turn to each other with looks and sighs of relief

Guzzle Chocolate pudding with rum sauce.
Gazer A touch of lavender water.
Gloom Epsom salts.
Gossip Ask no questions.

Thump There!
Twitting What did I say?
Thump There. There!

The Ladies turn to the door

The Wild One stands there

Wild One I can't. I can't leave you. No more than I could abandon you to a sinking ship or burning house. You're in danger here.

During the following speech The Wild One moves towards the Ladies. As she does so, the Ladies move from her, until they can go no farther. Then they move in the opposite direction, but still avoiding the open door. The result is a pendulum-like movement, with the Ladies moving to and fro

You'll die. Yes, it's a comfortable death, like being smothered with rose petals, but death is death however it comes. I'm telling you you'll die here. The worst kind of death—where the spirit dies first and the husk goes on clack-clack-clacking after. There are parasites that eat their victims from within until nothing is left but the outer skin: all that remains is a parody of life. Do you want that to happen to you? You're not dead yet, but you're sick, sick, sick. There's hope for you out there. You'll recover in the fresh air. Come with me, please. Please. I'm asking you. I'm pleading. Please. Please. Please.

They all come to a halt again. Pause

Why must I have a conscience? I could have been miles away by now. In safety. All right. If not all at once, then one at a time. (*She crosses to The Gloom*) You!

The Gloom gives a little cry, and tries to dodge out of her way, but only succeeds in becoming detached from the rest of the group

Come with me.

Gloom Oh, my cramp! (*Stamping back to the group*) When it takes me I can't put a foot to the ground. The muscles knot. Can't move an inch. If I were drowning, I'd have to stay put.

Wild One I could weep for you. (*She turns to The Guzzle*) There's nothing to fear out there.

Guzzle Don't talk to me about Irish Stew.

Wild One Nothing to hurt you,

Guzzle Welsh Rarebit.

Wild One I risked everything to come back for you.

Guzzle Scotch Broth neither.

Wild One If I'm caught, I'll be locked away again, and I can't live away from wild things.

Guzzle French mustard.

Wild One Come with me.

Guzzle Frankfurters and hamburgers.

Wild One Just as far as the door. Just to glimpse the free world outside. Just sniff the unpolluted air. Taste the wild honey.

Guzzle Honey?

Wild One Out there the fruit drops into your hand from the tree.

Guzzle Fruit!

Wild One (*backing towards the door and beckoning*) Apples, pears, plums, cherries. And green leaves fresh-washed with dew.

Guzzle Greens! (*She follows The Wild One as though hypnotized*)

Wild One The earth and its abundance is waiting for you. This way. This way. There.

The Guzzle reaches the door. She peers out. Then she shrieks, and runs back to the group

What am I doing here? You're not worth saving.

Guzzle Too much. Too many. Too big. Too far.

Wild One You could stretch your wings and fly. But you cling to your cage. Why? Why? Why?

Gossip Naturally, as I said to her—knowing where that story came from . . . (*She pauses, then carries on in a different voice. The words come slowly, almost painfully, as though dragged from her; and for the rest of the speech she alternates between her usual babble and this unusual speech. The effect is of two people talking*) Who—would—feed—us—out—there? . . . A likely tale, as I told her at the time. . . . Who—would—clothe—us—and—change—our—bathwater? . . . As if I hadn't known the whole family from the cradle on, as if she didn't know. . . . Who—would—protect—and—shelter—us—out there?

Wild One Out there you can take care of yourselves. Come and go as you please. This is a prison.

Gossip Our—prison.

Thump Ours.

Gloom Ours.

Gossip If—this—is—a—prison—it—is—well kept—and—clean.

Wild One A prison is a prison. All prisons should be destroyed. All cages broken open.

Gossip This—is—what—we—are—used—to. This—is—our—home.

Thump Ours.

Gloom Ours.

Guzzle Ours.

Wild One That's only what a cage has done to you. You'll sing a different song when you're over the fields and under the sky.

Gossip We—shall—stay.

Wild One No. I'll take you from this place if I have to burn it down. I'll march you lot to freedom, or die in the attempt.

Gossip Die.

Gloom Die.

Thump Die.

Guzzle Die.

Gazer Die.

They form a semicircle round The Wild One

Mistress (*off*) Who opened the door?

Wild One Too late, she's coming back.

Twitting She's come back. She's come back. She's come back.

Wild One She's not important. She can die. There are seven of us to one of her. And I opened the door for you. Kill her, and you'll all be free. Kill her!

The Ladies close in around The Wild One until she is hidden

Kill her and follow me! Kill her and destroy this cage! Kill——

(*She ends with a choking cry*)

Silence

The Mistress appears in the doorway

Mistress Who opened the door?

The Ladies scatter, leaving The Thump, who has her hands around The Wild One's neck. The Thump releases The Wild One, who slumps to the ground

Thump (*moving away*) There's too much violence in the news-papers these days.

Mistress What have you done? (*She comes down to The Wild One, and looks at the body*)

The Ladies all pretend to be concerned with something else, frantically establishing alibis

Guzzle White sauce covers a multitude of sins.

Gazer Why should anyone grow old?

Gloom It's my breathing, you know. Congestion.

Gossip I told them straight. That's your story, I said.

Twitting I know nothing. Nothing at all.

The Mistress looks up

Mistress Silly sweeties. Couldn't you understand her song? Poor little Wild One. We'll bury you in the garden. Will you be happy there? (*She goes up to the door*) Leave her alone while I fetch help to take her away. A pity. Given time, I'm sure she'd have grown to love her cage as much as you do. Such a pity.

The Mistress goes out and shuts the door behind her

Twitting I don't know. I really don't know. Everything seems to happen so suddenly these days. So confusing. (*She flutters over to the body, and looks down at it*) If only I could make up my mind. (*She kneels down by the body*) Destroy the cage, she said. There's nothing to fear out there. There's hope for you out there. Come with me, she said. This way. This way.

The Ladies exchange alarmed glances, then slowly, quietly begin to close in on The Twitting

Any door can be opened, she said. I'm offering you the world and you're afraid to take it. Out there is where the wind blows and the sun shines. Do you remember the clouds? Can you remember that and be content with this? She said. You could stretch your wings and fly. (*She looks up to see the Ladies around her in a semicircle*) I don't know. I don't know anything at all. I don't know. I don't know. I don't know. I don't know . . .

CURTAIN

FURNITURE AND PROPERTY LIST

On stage: 6 seats

Off stage: Small macaroon **(The Mistress)**

Personal: **Gazer:** compact mirror
Twitting: hairpin

LIGHTING PLOT

Property fittings required: nil
A room

To open: Overall rather cold lighting, with slightly sinister shadows

No cues

EFFECTS PLOT

Cue 1   **Twitting** "... when everything is always chang-
          ing?"   (Page 5)
          Pause, then amplified sound of key being turned in
          lock

Cue 2   **Mistress** exits   (Page 8)
          Repeat Cue 1

Roe Royce

"Love don't live here
anymore"

MADE AND PRINTED IN GREAT BRITAIN BY
LATIMER TREND & COMPANY LTD PLYMOUTH

MADE IN ENGLAND